SCHOLASTIC

READ & RESPOND

Bringing the best books to life in the classroom

Activities based on

Owl Babies

By Martin Waddell

Terms and conditions

IMPORTANT – PERMITTED USE AND WARNINGS – READ CAREFULLY BEFORE USING

This CD-ROM has been tested for viruses at all stages of its production. However, we recommend that you run virus-checking software on your computer systems at all times. Scholastic Ltd cannot accept any responsibility for any loss, disruption or damage to your data or your computer system that may occur as a result of using either the CD-ROM or the data held on it.

IF YOU ACCEPT THE ABOVE CONDITIONS YOU MAY PROCEED TO USE THE CD-ROM.

Recommended system requirements:

Windows: XP (Service Pack 3), Vista (Service Pack 2), Windows 7 or Windows 8 with 2.33GHz processor

Mac: OS 10.6 to 10.8 with Intel Core™ Duo processor

1GB RAM (recommended)

1024 × 768 Screen resolution

CD-ROM drive (24× speed recommended)

Adobe Reader (version 9 recommended for Mac users)

Broadband internet connections (for installation and updates)

For all technical support queries (including no CD drive), please phone Scholastic Customer Services on 0845 6039091.

Designed using Adobe Indesign
Published by Scholastic Education, an imprint of Scholastic Ltd
Book End, Range Road, Witney, Oxfordshire, OX29 0YD
Registered office: Westfield Road, Southam, Warwickshire CV47 0RA

Printed and bound by Ashford Colour Press

1 2 3 4 5 6 7 8 9 7 8 9 0 1 2 3 4 5 6

British Library Cataloguing-in-Publication Data
A catalogue record for this book is available from the British Library.
ISBN 978-1407-16052-8

Author Jean Evans
Editorial team Rachel Morgan, Jenny Wilcox, Suzanne Adams and Jennie Clifford
Series designer Neil Salt
Designer Anna Oliwa
Illustrator Gemma Hastilow
Digital development Hannah Barnett, Phil Crothers and MWA Technologies Private Ltd

Acknowledgements
The publishers gratefully acknowledge permission to reproduce the following copyright material:

Walker Books Ltd for permission to use the cover and text from 'Owl Babies' by Martin Waddell & Illustrated by Patrick Benson. Text © 1992 Martin Waddell. Illustrations © 1992 Patrick Benson. Reproduced by permission of Walker Books Ltd, London SE11 5HJ. www.walker.co.uk

Every effort has been made to trace copyright holders for the works reproduced in this book, and the publishers apologise for any inadvertent omissions.

CONTENTS

INTRODUCTION

Read & Respond provides teaching ideas related to a specific children's book. The series focuses on best-loved books and brings you ways to use them to engage your class and enthuse them about reading.

The book is divided into different sections.

- **About the book and author:** gives you some background information about the book and the author.
- **Guided reading:** breaks the book down into sections and gives notes for using it with guided reading groups. A bookmark has been provided on page 10 containing comprehension questions. The children can be directed to refer to these as they read.
- **Shared reading:** provides extracts from the children's book with associated notes for focused work. There is also one non-fiction extract that relates to the children's book.
- **Phonics & spelling:** provides phonics and spelling work related to the children's book so you can teach these skills in context.
- **Plot, character & setting:** contains activity ideas focused on the plot, characters and the setting of the story.
- **Talk about it:** has speaking and listening activities related to the children's book. These activities may be based directly on the children's book or be broadly based on the themes and concepts of the story.
- **Get writing:** provides writing activities related to the children's book. These activities may be based directly on the children's book or be broadly based on the themes and concepts of the story.
- **Assessment:** contains short activities that will help you assess whether the children have understood concepts and curriculum objectives. They are designed to be informal activities to feed into your planning.

The activities follow the same format.

- **Objective:** the objective for the lesson. It will be based upon a curriculum objective, but will often be more specific to the focus being covered.
- **What you need:** a list of resources you need to teach the lesson, including digital resources (printable pages, interactive activities and media resources, see page 5).
- **What to do:** the activity notes.
- **Differentiation:** this is provided where specific and useful differentiation advice can be given to support and/or extend the learning in the activity. Differentiation by providing additional adult support has not been included as this will be at a teacher's discretion based upon specific children's needs and ability, as well as the availability of support.

The activities are numbered for reference within each section and should move through the text sequentially – so you can use the lesson while you are reading the book. Once you have read the book, most of the activities can be used in any order you wish.

Below are brief guidance notes for using the CD-ROM. For more detailed information, please click on the '?' button in the top right-hand corner of the screen.

The program contains:

- the extract pages from the book
- all of the photocopiable pages from the book
- additional printable pages
- interactive on-screen activities
- media resources.

Getting started

Put the CD-ROM into your CD-ROM drive. If you do not have a CD-ROM drive, phone Scholastic Customer Services on 0845 6039091.

- For Windows users, the install wizard should autorun. If it fails to do so, then navigate to your CD-ROM drive. Then follow the installation process.
- For Mac users, copy the disk image file to your hard drive. After it has finished copying, double-click it to mount the disk image. Navigate to the mounted disk image and run the installer. After installation the disk image can be unmounted and the DMG can be deleted from the hard drive.
- To install on a network, see the ReadMe file located on the CD-ROM (navigate to your drive).

To complete the installation of the program, you need to open the program and click 'Update' in the pop-up. Please note – this CD-ROM is web-enabled and the content will be downloaded from the internet to your hard drive to populate the CD-ROM with the relevant resources. This only needs to be done on first use; after this you will be able to use the CD-ROM without an internet connection. If at any point any content is updated, you will receive another pop-up upon start-up when there is an internet connection.

Main menu

The Main menu is the first screen that appears. Here you can access: terms and conditions, registration links, how to use the CD-ROM, and credits. To access a specific book, click on the relevant button. (Note only titles installed will be available.) You can filter by the drop-down lists if you wish. You can search all resources by clicking 'Search' in the bottom left-hand corner. You can also log in and access favourites that you have bookmarked.

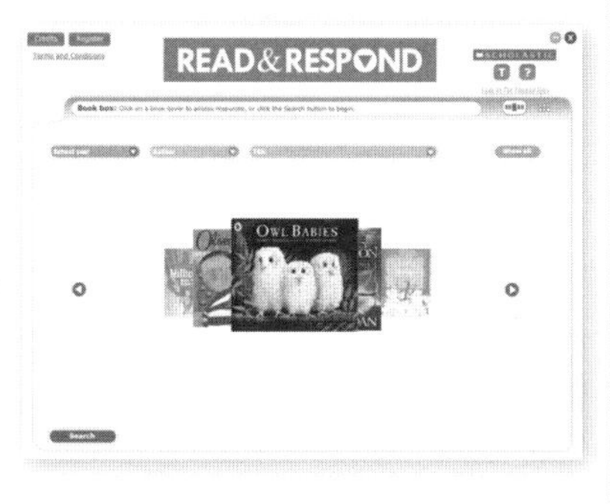

Resources

By clicking on a book on the Main menu, you are taken to the resources for that title. The resources are: Media, Interactives, Extracts, and Printables. Select the category and then launch a resource by clicking the 'Play' button.

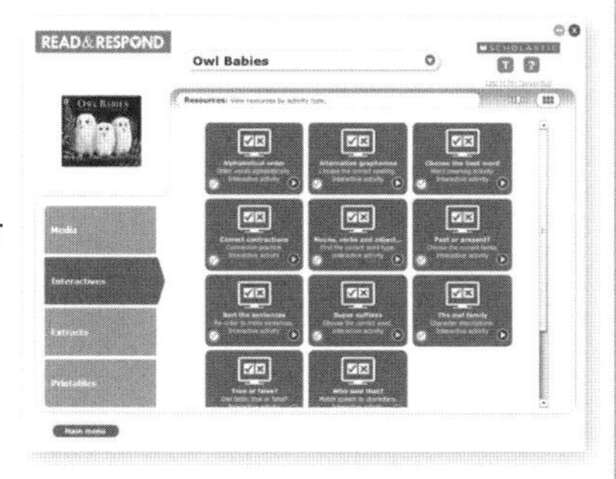

Teacher settings

In the top right-hand corner of the screen is a small 'T' icon. This is the teacher settings area. It is password protected, and the password is: login. This area will allow you to choose the print quality settings for interactive activities ('Default' or 'Best') and also allow you to check for updates to the program or re-download all content to the disk via 'Refresh all content'. You can also set up user logins so that you can save and access favourites. Once a user is set up, they can enter by clicking the login link underneath the 'T' and '?' buttons.

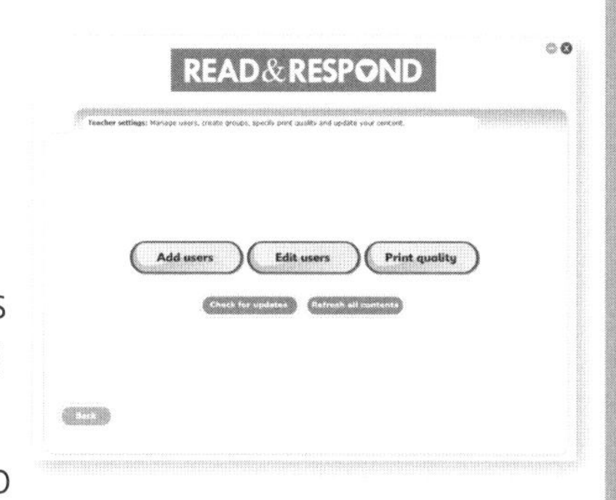

Search

You can access an all-resources search by clicking the 'Search' button on the bottom left of the Main menu. You can search for activities by type (using the drop-down filter) or by keyword by typing into the box. You can then assign resources to your favourites area or launch them directly from the search area.

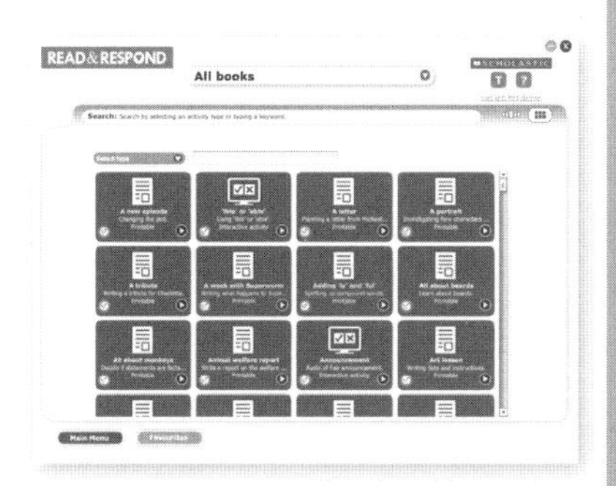

CURRICULUM LINKS

Section	Activity	Curriculum objectives
Guided reading		Comprehension: To participate in discussion about what is read to them, taking turns and listening to what others say; to explain clearly their understanding of what is read to them.
Shared reading	1	Comprehension: To draw on what they already know or on background information and vocabulary provided by the teacher.
	2	Composition: To learn how to use familiar and new punctuation correctly.
	3	Comprehension: To discuss word meanings, linking new meanings to those already known.
Phonics	1	Word reading: To read words containing taught GPCs and 's', 'es', 'ing', 'ed', 'er' and 'est' endings.
	2	Word reading: To respond speedily with the correct sound to graphemes (letters or groups of letters) for all 40+ phonemes, including, where applicable, alternative sounds for graphemes.
	3	Word reading: To read words with contractions (for example I'm, I'll, we'll), and understand that the apostrophe represents the omitted letter(s).
	4	Word reading: To read common exception words, noting unusual correspondences between spelling and sound and where these occur in the word.
Plot, character & setting	1	Comprehension: To become very familiar with key stories, fairy stories and traditional tales, retelling them and considering their particular characteristics.
	2	Comprehension: To draw on what they already know or on background information and vocabulary provided by the teacher.
	3	Comprehension: To link what they read or hear read to their own experiences.
	4	Composition: To sequence sentences to form short narratives.
	5	Comprehension: To make inferences on the basis of what is being said and done.
	6	Comprehension: To discuss word meanings, linking new meanings to those already known.
Talk about it	1	Spoken language: To participate in discussions, presentations, performances, role play, improvisations and debates.
	2	Spoken language: To participate in discussions, presentations, performances, role play, improvisations and debates.
	3	Comprehension: To recognise and join in with predictable phrases.
	4	Spoken language: To maintain attention and participate actively in collaborative conversations, staying on topic and initiating and responding to comments.
	5	Spoken language: To consider and evaluate different viewpoints, attending to and building on the contributions of others.
	6	Spoken language: To give well-structured explanations and narratives for different purposes, including for expressing feelings.
Get writing	1	Composition: To discuss what they have written with the teacher or other pupils.
	2	Composition: To say out loud what they are going to write about.
	3	Transcription: To spell the days of the week.
	4	Transcription: To begin to form lower-case letters in the correct direction, starting and finishing in the right place; to form capital letters.
	5	Composition: To read aloud their writing clearly enough to be heard by peers and the teacher.
	6	Composition: To sequence sentences to form short narratives.
Assessment	1	Transcription: To name the letters of the alphabet in order.
	2	Composition: To use the grammatical terminology in English Appendix 2 in discussing their writing.
	3	Word reading: To apply phonic knowledge and skills as the route to decode words.
	4	Composition: To re-read what they have written to check that it makes sense; to learn how to use the present and past tenses correctly and consistently.

About the book

Owl Babies is a charming story about three baby owls, Sarah, Percy and Bill, who wake up in their nest one night to find their mother has gone. The youngest baby, Bill, is distraught and begins to cry for his mummy, while the other two try their best to comfort him. Young children sharing this story will undoubtedly empathise with the plight of these young owls as they recall occasions when they have been left without the reassurance of a familiar adult, perhaps on their first day at school. Martin Waddell's words, and the superb expressive detail in Patrick Benson's illustrations, help children to come to terms with their own feelings as they share the highs and lows of emotion experienced by the little owls. The children discover more about sibling relationships as they observe the sensible older sister caring for her younger brothers, the middle baby trying his best to appear brave in front of the others and the youngest baby naturally turning to his sister for reassurance. This is a wonderful story, with a happy ending that will inspire warm feelings of belonging.

About the author

Martin Waddell is widely acknowledged as one of the most popular writers of children's books, and is probably best known for his engaging picture books. His *Big Bear, Little Bear* series is loved by children around the world. He also writes for older children – mainly ghost stories and mystery fiction. Martin was born in Ireland in 1941 and still lives there with his wife. He dreams up stories in his garden, writes in an old barn and enjoys long walks along the beach in front of his house. As a boy, Martin loved playing football and later signed for Fulham, where he was a goalkeeper. After realising that he would not have a career as a professional player, he turned to writing. His love of this sport is reflected in his series of books about a football-playing boy called Napper.

About the illustrator

Patrick Benson studied classical drawing in Florence and attended Chelsea Art School. His career was in fashion until he met the sister of Sebastian Walker who introduced him to Walker Books. Since then he has illustrated books for a variety of authors, and is best known for his illustrations of *Owl Babies* by Martin Waddell and *The Minpins* by Roald Dahl. He won the Mother Goose Award as the most promising newcomer in children's book illustration in 1984, and has had books shortlisted for the Kate Greenaway Medal. *The Little Boat* won the 1995 Kurt Maschler Award.

Key facts

Owl Babies

Author: Martin Waddell

Illustrator: Patrick Benson

First published: 1992 by Walker Books

Did you know?: Martin's books for young children have won many awards, including the Smarties Book Prize (twice), the British Book Awards Children's Illustrated Book of the Year, Best Babies' Book of the Year, the Kurt Maschler Award and the Hans Christian Andersen Award for contribution to children's literature.

Cover clues

Show the children the front cover of the book. Invite them to focus on the text and illustration and make predictions about the possible content. Read the title together and ask question 1 on the Guided Reading bookmark (page 10). Ask question 2 and discuss the children's responses. Talk about the owl features that the babies exhibit, such as huge eyes and sharp, pointed beaks. If necessary, point out the fluffy feathers indicating that they are babies.

Invite children to point to the names of the author and illustrator, Martin Waddell and Patrick Benson, and establish which is which. To extend this discussion, find more about the author and illustrator on page 7 of this book.

Explore the background surrounding the babies and identify clues, such as the branch and leaves, and the dark background indicating where and when the story might be set (in a tree during the night). Turn to the back cover and read the first line together. Discuss how this helps to confirm the setting for the story. Read the rest of this paragraph and speculate on what might happen next. Ask question 7 on the bookmark to establish the names of the story characters, and revise the importance of using capital letters for names.

Having explored the front and back covers, ask question 3 on the bookmark to establish who the children think are the main characters. Recall other stories that have a group of significant characters rather than one main one.

Spreads 1 to 3

Read spreads 1 to 3, ensuring that your initial reading of *Owl Babies* awakens the children's emotions and builds upon their initial impressions, without making them too upset over the plight of the owls. Read with expression, raising and lowering your voice for dramatic effect and to add atmosphere, for example, emphasising the word 'GONE', taking a small gasp afterwards and cupping your hand over your mouth in shock. Vary the voices of the owls, defining their characters with a confident tone for Sarah, a brave but questioning tone for Percy and a tiny squeak for Bill. Make effective use of the varying punctuation clues, for example, raising your voice when words are in capitals ('GONE'), emphasising words when exclamation marks are present ('I want my mummy!') and whispering dramatically when words are in italics ('The baby owls *thought*'). Vary vocal tone and body language to build up mood and atmosphere (for instance, peering around and whispering when reading emotive words or phrases such as 'Oh my goodness!'). Indicate words by moving along them with a finger or pointer as you read. Remember to pause at significant points to ask questions about what might happen next. Continue to apply these methods throughout the story.

Ask question 4 on the bookmark and look at how the text and illustrations confirm children's predictions that the story takes place in a tree. Invite children to share what they know about birds and their nests, and look again at the illustrations on spreads 1 and 2, which depict the inside of the owl house. Notice that the author refers to the owl home as a house rather than a nest. Ask the children what the text tells us about the position of the house and the way it is constructed. Consider the natural materials employed by the owls to make their house comfortable. Speculate on why the house is in a hole in a tree.

Focus on the conversation of the owls as they discuss their mother's disappearance and encourage the children to suggest where they think Owl Mother has gone and what might happen next.

Spreads 4 to 8

Read spreads 4 to 8 and focus on the words of Bill, the smallest baby owl ('I want my mummy!'). Invite the children to indicate every time they hear Bill speak as you read, and then repeat his words. Ask question 10 to encourage children to discuss times when they have felt worried without the presence of their mother or a familiar adult. Perhaps they lost sight of Mum for a short while in a shop, or woke suddenly from a frightening dream? Ask question 5 on the Guided Reading bookmark to establish how the owls are feeling as they consider worrying things that might happen to their mother and decide what to do (sit together on Sarah's branch and wait – spread 7). Did the children feel the same when they were alone? Discuss the importance of talking through problems together. Extend the discussion to include consideration about the strength of relationships and the importance of caring for one another. Always be prepared to deal sensitively with the children's comments about their experiences.

Look together at how the owl babies resort to closing their eyes and wishing (spread 8).

Spreads 9 to 12

Read spreads 9 to 12, using your voice to create drama as you read the words 'AND SHE CAME' (spread 9). As you continue to read, ensure that children focus on individual words in the text through appropriate comments and queries. For instance, ask question 8 on the Guided Reading Bookmark to focus on the use of effective adjectives that describe bird movements. Ask question 6 to establish that Bill repeats his words throughout the story but changes them at the end when his mother returns. Talk about why Bill has few words, and compare his use of language with that of very young children the children know.

Re-read the story and discuss how it is structured. Establish that it has a clear beginning, with the owls finding themselves alone, and a definite end, when their mother returns. Discuss what happens in the middle.

Draw attention to the detailed owl illustrations and discuss how they enhance the story. Explore the expressions on the baby owls' faces and their body language as they discuss their plight, wait patiently and finally bounce up and down eagerly on their mother's return. Ask question 9 on the bookmark to initiate discussion about whether the illustrator has effectively conveyed how the owls are feeling through these images. Finally, encourage children to voice their initial impressions of the book.

SCHOLASTIC

READ&RESPOND

Bringing the best books to life in the classroom

Owl Babies
by Martin Waddell

Focus on…
Meaning

1. What do you think the story might be about? Does the title help with your answer?
2. Do you think the birds on the front cover are the owl babies in the title? What makes you think this?
3. Do you think there is one main character in the story, or more than one? Why do you think this?

Focus on…
Organisation

4. What sort of setting does the story take place in? What clues do the text and illustrations provide to help you with your answer?
5. How does the owls' conversation help the reader to understand what is in their minds and how they are feeling? What do they decide to do as a result of their discussion?
6. What do you notice about the words Bill uses? Why do they change at the end of the story?

SCHOLASTIC

READ&RESPOND

Bringing the best books to life in the classroom

Owl Babies
by Martin Waddell

Focus on…
Language and features

7. What do you notice about the first letters of the names of the owl babies and Owl Mother?
8. Do you think the words 'soft', 'silent', 'swoop', 'flap' and 'bounce' describe owl movements well? Can you think of similar words the author might have used?

Focus on…
Purpose, viewpoints and effects

9. How do you think the expressions on the faces of the baby owls, and the way they are moving, help us understand how they are feeling at different points in the story?
10. Have you ever felt lost or alone? What did you do? Do you think the owls knew that their mother would come back to them?

Extract 1

- Display Extract 1 on page 12. Invite children to identify story language indicating that this is the opening page ('Once there were...'). Discuss information given about the characters and setting. Recall bookmark question 3, and ask whether the extract provides further evidence to back up or change the children's original responses.
- Refer to the previous owl house discussion ('Guided reading' section for spreads 1 to 3) and highlight the words 'hole', 'trunk', 'tree', 'twigs', 'leaves' and 'owl feathers'. Discuss the role these words play in creating a 'mind's eye' image of the owl house. Ask children to compose sentences to describe the owls' house using these words. Think of an alternative word for a bird house that could have been used ('nest'). Do the children prefer the word 'nest' or 'house' in this context?
- Circle the capital letters and discuss the reasons for using them. Question why the word 'owl' has a capital letter alongside 'Mother', but not otherwise.

Extract 2

- Display Extract 2 and establish that it is the last page of the book. Discuss whether the story has an effective ending, and why.
- Focus on punctuation. Consider why Owl Mother's words are in capitals. Recall previous experience of words being in capitals for emphasis. Invite individuals to take turns to read the first sentence, emphasising the words in capitals loudly. Try reading them quietly and then with the same volume for the whole sentence. Do either of these options work as well? Invite children to recall when adults speak loudly to them, perhaps to get their attention, and then decide why Owl Mother was speaking loudly in this instance.
- Circle the inverted commas and highlight the exclamation marks and question mark. Revise the use of these punctuation marks. Explain that the brackets are used when extra information is added inside a sentence. Establish the information that has been added in this instance ('all owls think a lot').

Extract 3

- Display an enlarged copy of Extract 3 with only the heading showing. Ask whether the children think the page is fiction or non-fiction, giving reasons for their choice. If necessary, highlight the word 'facts' and establish that this indicates non-fiction.
- Display the whole page and establish that the words in bold are printed in boxes below. Divide the class into ten small groups and ask each group to read out a different fact in turn. Ask the rest of the class to support them with reading the words in bold. Invite the groups to decide which fact is their favourite, and to explain why they have chosen this one.
- Return to the bold words in the list and ensure, by discussion and explanation, that the children understand the meaning of each one. Now cover the fact list and ask the children to try to recall the meaning of these words.

Extract 1

Once there were three baby owls:
Sarah and Percy and Bill.
They lived in a hole
in the trunk of a tree
with their Owl Mother.
The hole had twigs and
leaves and owl feathers in it.
It was their house.

One night they woke up and
their Owl Mother was GONE.
"Where's Mummy?" asked Sarah.
"Oh my goodness!" said Percy.
"I want my mummy!" said Bill.

Extract 2

"WHAT'S ALL THE FUSS?"
their Owl Mother asked.
"You knew I'd come back."
The baby owls thought
(all owls think a lot) –
"I knew it," said Sarah.
"And I knew it!" said Percy.
"I love my mummy!" said Bill.

Extract 3

Ten amazing owl facts

1. Owls are **nocturnal**, which means they are active at night.

2. Owls eat insects and small **mammals** such as **rodents**.

3. Some owls even eat worms, small birds and fish.

4. Owls have very powerful hearing so that they can hunt in darkness.

5. Owls have flat faces and large eyes that face forwards.

6. Owls are able to turn their heads a long way round to search for **prey**.

7. Owls have very sharp claws called **talons** to help catch and kill their prey, and sharp hooked beaks that they use to tear meat.

8. Owls are well **camouflaged** because their feathers are the same colour as their surroundings.

9. Some owls, such as the barn owl, are **endangered** and need protection.

10. A baby owl is called an **owlet**.

Interesting owl vocabulary

nocturnal prey talons owlet rodents
mammals camouflaged endangered

1. Super suffixes

Objective

To read words containing taught GPCs and 's', 'es', 'ing', 'ed', 'er' and 'est' endings.

What you need

Interactive activity 'Super suffixes', copies of *Owl Babies*, individual whiteboards.

What to do

- Revise the rule for adding the suffixes 'ing' and 'ed' to verbs, and 'er' and 'est' to adjectives (if the word ends in two consonant letters, the ending is simply added on). Provide examples on the board to demonstrate this.
- Revise the rule for plural endings (if the ending is pronounced /s/ or /z/ it is spelled 's'; if it is pronounced /iz/ it is spelled 'es'). Again, provide examples.
- Display the first screen of interactive activity 'Super suffixes'. Read the instruction together to establish that children understand that they need to choose the correct name from the drop-down box to complete each sentence.
- Complete the first sentence together.
- Display the second and third screens in turn and explain that this time the children need to choose the words with the correct endings. Again, complete a sentence from each one as an example.
- Allow time for individual completion of the whole activity before discussing the correct suffixes as a class.

Differentiation

Support: Complete only the screen(s) relevant to the child's current experience and ability.
Extension: Ask children to write a list of words in *Owl Babies* that end in 'ed' on their whiteboards (such as 'flapped' and 'closed'). Encourage them to identify the root words ('flap' and 'close') and explain the rule for adding 'ed' in each case.

2. Alternative graphemes

Objective

To respond speedily with the correct sound to graphemes.

What you need

Copies of *Owl Babies*, individual whiteboards, interactive activity 'Alternative graphemes'.

What to do

- Choose ten words from *Owl Babies* that contain previously learned graphemes, including some alternative pronunciations, such as 'sat', 'baby' and 'all' for the grapheme 'a'. Ask children to write each word on their whiteboards. Discuss the grapheme used to create the phoneme in each case.
- Display interactive activity 'Alternative graphemes'. Explain that the baby owls tried to write their story but could not decide how to spell some words so they put their spelling attempts in a box beside each sentence.
- Ask the children to help by identifying the correct word from each box and dragging and dropping this into place in the sentence.
- Complete the first sentence together. Discuss the spelling of the two remaining words. Ask: *What happens to the 'a' sound in 'baby' when another 'b' is added?*
- Do the same with the next sentence, drawing attention to the sound change for the letter 'o' in the words 'hole' and 'holl', identifying the nonsense word. Discuss the alternative phonemes that can be created by putting the letter 'o' alongside the letter 'w' and think of other words with this grapheme-phoneme correspondence ('trowel', 'now', 'cow').
- Ask children to complete the activity in pairs, reading aloud their completed sentences to check that they make sense.
- Invite the whole class to read the sequence of sentences together to tell the owls' story.

3. Creating contractions

Objective

To read words with contractions, and understand that the apostrophe represents the omitted letter(s).

What you need

Extract 2, printable page 'Create contractions', interactive activity 'Correct contractions'.

What to do

- Revise the meaning of 'contraction'.
- Display Extract 2 and ask children to find the contractions (WHAT'S, I'd), and say the words each contraction represents (WHAT IS, I would). Re-read the extract omitting the contractions. Ask which version they prefer.
- Explain that we often use contractions when we speak, and say: *We're going to write our own contractions using sentences I've made up.* Encourage the children to identify the contractions you used in your sentence ('We're' and 'I've').
- Display printable page 'Create contractions' and read the instructions together. Work through the first sentence on the board together as an example. Identify two words that can be shortened (Where is), which letter needs to be removed and where to insert an apostrophe.
- Display the first screen of interactive activity 'Correct contractions' and read the instruction. Explain that three spellings have been given for each contraction and the children must decide which is correct. Work an example together.
- Suggest that children work in pairs to complete both activities, discussing the options together.
- Bring children together to self-correct work as you complete the activities on the board.

Differentiation

Support: Encourage the children to complete the 'Create contractions' activity initially, only moving on to 'Correct contractions' if they are able.
Extension: Suggest that children compose sentences about the story using contractions.

4. Word games

Objective

To read common exception words, noting unusual correspondences and where these occur in the word.

What you need

Printable pages '*Owl Babies* lotto'.

What to do

- Cut out all the words from printable page '*Owl Babies* lotto'. There should be a set of word cards for each group (four).
- Display a game card, point to a regular word and invite the children to read it, discussing any phonic rules applied. Now choose a common exception word, such as 'once', and discuss why this is more difficult to read.
- Explain that you have made a word game to help children learn how to read the more difficult four-letter words from *Owl Babies*, as well as to revise the easier ones.
- Divide the children into groups of four, providing each group with a set of word cards and four game boards. Place the word cards upside down in the centre of the table.
- Invite one group member to take the top card, read the word aloud without showing the others and call out the first letter. The adjacent child should then call the next letter, and so on, until the word is spelled correctly. Another child then turns over the next word. If it is the same as the previous one, all four can call out the letters.
- Now play a regular lotto game using the word cards and game boards, with the children taking turns to turn over a word card. (Word list: eyes, said, dark, gone, here, hole, love, mice, move, once, owls, soon, they, tree, twig, want, were, woke, wood.)

1. Tell the story

Objective

To become familiar with key stories, retelling them and considering their characteristics.

What you need

Copies of *Owl Babies*, media resource 'Owl nests', cardboard boxes, natural materials including white wool, twigs, feathers, pine cones and leaves, polystyrene craft balls.

Cross-curricular links

Drama, art and design

What to do

- Read *Owl Babies* and ask the children to identify facts they have learned about owl nests from the text and illustrations. Explore the images and film clips in media resource 'Owl nests' to extend this knowledge.
- List owl facts on the board, for example, 'Owls build their nests in holes in trees'.
- Suggest that the children re-enact the story. Explain that they will need to make their own props representing the nest and characters.
- Remind children to refer to their facts list when deciding how things should look. Read this list together and discuss how it might help making the props. Perhaps you could discuss the possibility of making Owl Mother using a pine cone, the babies from clippings of white wool attached to polystyrene balls, and the nest by sticking natural materials such as leaves and twigs to the side of a box representing the tree-trunk hole.
- Divide the children into groups for prop-making.
- Drape green fabric over a table to represent a stage. Invite groups to re-enact the story to the class using the props they have made.
- Make a class decision about which group performed the most accurate dramatisation of the story.

2. Extending knowledge

Objective

To draw on what they already know or on information and vocabulary provided by the teacher.

What you need

Extract 3, copies of *Owl Babies*, media resources 'Tawny owls' and 'Owl nests', information from bird protection charities, owl trusts and sanctuaries, model owls and nests from previous activity.

Cross-curricular link

Science, art & design

What to do

- Recall the facts about owls and their nests discovered during the previous activity, and discuss the owl facts in Extract 3.
- Suggest the children create a classroom interactive display about owls and their lifestyle.
- Decide upon the key information categories they will explore and find out more about, for example, physical features, diet, habitat, lifestyle, species.
- Divide them into groups and assign a different category for each group to research. Provide a copy of *Owl Babies*, Extract 3, access to media resources 'Tawny owls' and 'Owl nests', and links to websites of various bird and owl charities.
- Encourage groups to collect information to extend their knowledge about their given category, and display this attractively to inform the rest of the class through posters, paintings and labelled artwork.
- Bring the class together and ask each group to present their information, referring to their artwork as they do so. After each presentation, encourage the class to ask questions and comment on the quality of information included.
- Create a large classroom display incorporating the children's owl models and nests, along with the artwork from this activity presented under the key category headings.

3. Family descriptions

Objective

To be encouraged to link what they read or hear read to their own experiences.

What you need

Copies of *Owl Babies*, interactive activity 'The owl family', large sheets of paper.

Cross-curricular link

PSHE

What to do

- Recall previous discussions about the *Owl Babies* family. Encourage children to make comparisons with their own families by asking appropriate questions, for example: *Who is Percy's brother? Who is Percy's sister?*
- Refer to the book's text and illustrations as you talk about how Owl Mother seems to be looking after her babies alone. Deal sensitively with any discussion arising about single-parent families.
- Focus on what we know about the owl characters, for example, Bill is more frightened than the others (perhaps because he is the youngest), and Sarah seems to be the bravest and most sensible. Encourage children to make comparisons with their siblings' characteristics.
- Display interactive activity 'The owl family'. Read each sentence together, deciding upon the character identified in each one. Ask children to describe similar characters in their own families.
- Provide large sheets of paper and writing materials. Ask children to draw their families, with each member in a separate box. Suggest that they write the name at the top of each box and appropriate adjectives underneath.

4. Storyboard sequences

Objective

To sequence sentences to form short narratives.

What you need

Photocopiable page 20 '*Owl Babies* storyboard', scissors, glue sticks, large sheets of paper divided into 8 boxes for storyboards, coloured pens, copies of *Owl Babies*.

Cross-curricular link

Mathematics

What to do

- Revise the children's understanding of story structure, referring to 'beginning', 'middle' and 'end', and discuss following a sequence.
- Talk about the structure of this story, beginning when the babies wake alone and ending when their mother returns, with the middle section focusing on the babies' discussion.
- Divide the board into three columns headed 'Beginning', 'Middle' and 'End' and invite children to choose key events to write in them.
- Display an enlarged version of photocopiable page 20 '*Owl Babies* storyboard'. Invite the children to decide whether each sentence occurs at the beginning, middle or end of the story.
- Explain what is involved in a storyboard. Discuss how to use the prepared paper to create a storyboard by cutting out the sentences, arranging them in the correct sequence and sticking them into the boxes in order. Explain that they will complete the storyboards by illustrating them.
- Divide them into groups, each with the photocopiable sheet and the resources listed above.
- Bring the class together to discuss the most interesting and accurate storyboard.

Differentiation

Support: Encourage children to refer to copies of *Owl Babies* when ordering the sentences.
Extension: Suggest that children create a storyboard for a favourite story.

5. Perfect perches

Objective

To make inferences on the basis of what is being said and done.

What you need

Children's dictionary, media resource 'Perching owls', short branches of varying widths, twigs, artificial ivy (do not let children handle real ivy), copies of *Owl Babies*, photocopiable page 21 'Perfect perches', coloured pens (including red and green).

Cross-curricular links

Mathematics, science

What to do

- Establish the meanings of the word 'perch' when used as a noun and a verb, reading a few dictionary definitions if necessary.
- Explore the images and film clips of owls on different perches in media resource 'Perching owls'. Focus on their long talons and discuss how they wrap them around the perch to steady themselves.
- Handle branches, twigs and artificial ivy (if you have them). Speculate on factors involved when owls decide to use them as perches (size, position, strength). Ask questions to encourage logical inference, for example, *What will happen if heavy owls perch on this thin twig? Why do owls perch high in trees? Would a sloping roof make a good perch?*
- Focus on the illustration of the owls perched on different branches (spread 5). Ask questions to encourage discussion about why they might have chosen those perches, for example, *What if Sarah tried sitting on Bill's ivy?*
- Display photocopiable page 21 'Perfect perches'. Ask children to read the first statement together, discuss whether it is true or false and give reasons for their answer. Colour the 'False' box red.
- Provide coloured pens and copies of the photocopiable sheet for children to complete.

6. Investigating dialogue

Objective

To discuss word meanings, linking new meanings to those already known.

What you need

Thick card, copies of *Owl Babies*, interactive activity 'Choose the best word', thick card.

What to do

- Prepare eight cards, each with an adjective describing an owl character's feelings during different parts of the story, such as 'curious', 'thoughtful', 'confident', 'worried', 'frightened', 'excited', 'happy', 'shocked'.
- Read the story to the children, focusing on dialogue. Discuss why the owls always speak in the same order: Bill repeats his words until the last page, and Percy takes his lead from Sarah's comments. Explore what this tells us about the owls' characters.
- Divide the children into groups, each with a word card. Ask them to read the word and discuss its meaning.
- Invite groups to read their word to the class and explain its meaning.
- Choose sentences of dialogue to read to the class. Ask groups to hold up their word if it describes the character's feeling when he/she said this. If more than one card is held up, discuss which is most appropriate.
- Display interactive activity 'Choose the best word' and read the instructions. Complete the first one together, giving a reason for the chosen word.
- Ask children to work in pairs, discussing word meanings before choosing the most appropriate.

Differentiation

Support: Focus on supporting children's understanding of the word meanings before starting the lesson.
Extension: Invite children to compose sentences about their own feelings using the words on the cards.

Owl Babies storyboard

- Cut out the boxes so that you have eight sentences.
- Arrange the sentences in the correct sequence to tell the story.

They talked about when their mother would come back.	Once there lived three baby owls and a mother owl.
And she came!	Then they all moved to the same branch.
They talked about where their mother might be.	They closed their eyes and wished their mother was back.
They left the nest and sat on three different branches.	One night the babies woke up and their mother had gone.

Perfect perches

- Read the statement in each box.
- Decide whether the statement is true or false.
- Colour in the correct box beside it, using green for true and red for false.

Statement		
Percy sat on the biggest branch in the tree.	True	False
Bill sat on a bit of old ivy.	True	False
Sarah sat on a wall.	True	False
Sarah's branch was higher than Percy's.	True	False
Percy's branch was lower than Bill's ivy.	True	False
Sarah sat on the strongest branch because she was the heaviest.	True	False
Sarah was at the top, Percy was in the middle and Bill was at the bottom.	True	False
Percy perched above Sarah and below Bill.	True	False

TALK ABOUT IT

1. Owl stick puppets

Objective

To participate in discussions, role play and improvisations.

What you need

Copies of *Owl Babies*, photocopiable page 25 'How to make owl baby puppets', printable page 'Owl templates', scissors, card, glue, sticky tape, 20cm lengths of thin dowelling, white wool, small googly eyes, yellow felt, cardboard tubes with 3 pairs of holes at even intervals cut so that the dowelling will slide through (see photocopiable page 25), example of a finished owl puppet.

Cross-curricular links

Design & technology, drama

What to do

- Explore the illustrations of the babies sitting on the same branch on the front cover and inside *Owl Babies*. Discuss what they might be saying to one another as they wait anxiously for their mother.
- Explain that they are going to re-enact this scene, with dialogue, using puppets they will be making.
- Display photocopiable page 25 'How to make owl baby puppets'. Read the title and establish that it is a non-fiction instruction sheet.
- Pass around the finished puppet before reading and discussing the page together.
- Suggest that the children work in pairs. Provide them with printable page 'Owl templates', along with the materials they need, then give support while they make their puppets.
- Bring the class together to demonstrate how to slot the puppets through the holes on a cardboard tube so that they 'sit on the branch'.
- The pairs can then re-enact their scene, with one child holding the tube and a puppet while the other holds two puppets. The puppets can be moved to bounce up and down on the branch using the dowelling.

2. Sounds of the night

Objective

To participate in discussions and performances.

What you need

Copies of *Owl Babies*, media resource 'Night sounds, sound-making objects such as dry leaves, thin fabric, cellophane, percussion and musical instruments (for example, a rainstick or an ocarina).

Cross-curricular link

Drama

What to do

- Read *Owl Babies* and talk about when the story takes place (night time).
- Invite the children to sit on the floor, close their eyes and imagine they are owl babies sitting on a branch in the tree. Listen to the recorded sound effects in media resource 'Night sounds' and discuss their possible origins.
- Ask them to suggest some more night sounds that they might hear as they sit on the branch (shuffling hedgehogs, squeaking mice, barking foxes).
- Make a list of woodland night sounds on the board and discuss ways of creating them, for example, small creatures squeaking and shuffling (voices or scrunching cellophane), owls hooting (voice or instruments such as an ocarina or recorder), birds' wings (flapping fabric), wind (swishing grasses), wolf or fox (voice); owls shuffling along the branch (sandpaper blocks).
- Divide the children into groups to explore tables of instruments, natural materials and everyday objects. Ask them to take turns to make suggestions about using items for sound effects while the others listen before making comments.
- Ask each group to perform their chosen sound effects while individual members narrate different sections of the story.
- Extend the activity by creating sound effects for different weather conditions in the woods that night, such as rain, thunder and wind.

3. Owl conversations

Objective

To recognise and join in with predictable phrases.

What you need

Copies of *Owl Babies*, interactive activity 'Who said that?'

What to do

- Read the story and invite children to recall previous discussions about the owl babies' conversation when it was established who speaks first, second and third in each sequence.
- Read the words of Sarah and Percy on the second spread, pausing for children to join in with Bill's words, 'I want my mummy!'
- Do the same with dialogue on the next page, encouraging children to join in with Percy's words as well, if they can.
- Continue in this way until the last spread. Ask children what they have to remember about Bill's words on this page before reading it ('want' is replaced by 'love').
- Display screen 1 of interactive activity 'Who said that?' and explain that you have made up sentences that the owl babies might have said. Read the instructions together.
- Ask the children which owl they think will say the same words in every sentence sequence (Bill), which owl will always say the first sentence (Sarah) and which owl will say the second (Percy).
- Complete the first sequence of sentences together before asking children to complete the activity in pairs.

Differentiation

Support: Encourage children to focus on Bill's repeated words and to realise what is different about his words in the last sequence of sentences.
Extension: Ask children to compose their own predictable sequences of sentences for the baby owls.

4. Owl Mother went hunting

Objective

To maintain attention and participate actively in collaborative conversations.

What you need

Sand tray, leaves and twigs, model creatures owls like to eat (such as worms, mice, insects, spiders, frogs, small birds, lizards, snails), copies of *Owl Babies*, Extract 3.

Cross-curricular link

Science

What to do

- Prepare a sand tray to represent the forest floor by scattering leaves and twigs across the bottom and hiding model creatures amongst them.
- Ask the children to sit in a circle with the tray in the centre. Read *Owl Babies* and discuss the things that Owl Mother might bring back for her hungry babies when she goes hunting.
- Display Extract 3 and read this to find further evidence of things that owls eat.
- Recall the memory game 'I went to the shop and I bought...' and explain that this game is played in the same way.
- Start the game by pulling a creature out of the tray and saying: *Owl Mother went hunting tonight and caught a worm.*
- Invite a child to pull something out and continue the game as follows: *...a worm and a [mouse].*
- Continue until the children can no longer remember the sequence. Make a note of how many creatures have been memorised and see if this number increases with subsequent games.

Differentiation

Extension: Ask children to create alliterative descriptions of creatures caught, for example, 'a squishy, squashy worm', 'a fat, furry mouse'.

5. Owl Mother action

Objective

To consider and evaluate different viewpoints.

What you need

Copies of *Owl Babies*, printable page 'What makes a good owl mother? (1), printable page 'What makes a good owl mother? (2).

Cross-curricular link

PSHE

What to do

- Read the story to the class and invite them to consider the actions of Owl Mother.
- Read the phrase 'all owls think a lot' and suggest that the children try to think like owls for this activity. Explain that owls are very wise and so the children will need to think carefully about the questions you are going to ask them!
- Display printable page 'What makes a good owl mother (1)?' and ask the children to decide how an owl would answer the questions. Ask the first question, decide on a class answer and write this on the board.
- Display printable page 'What makes a good owl mother? (2)'. Explain that these questions are specifically for Owl Mother and so they should try to think like this character, recalling her actions from the story to help them.
- Divide the class into groups of four, each with a copy of both printable pages. Ask two children to discuss and work together to agree answers to printable page 'What makes a good owl mother? (1)', and two to do the same for printable page 'What makes a good owl mother? (2)'.
- Once they have completed their pages, they can compare their responses to the numbered questions and work as a group to come to joint decisions about answers.
- Bring the class together to share their answers. Ask: *Did you find that the answers to both pages were similar?* Talk about how knowing owl facts helped with some answers.

6. In the hot seat

Objective

To give explanations for different purposes, including for expressing feelings.

What you need

Owl baby name cards, ribbon, large pet basket, cushions, copies of *Owl Babies*, individual whiteboards.

Cross-curricular link

PSHE

What to do

- Attach the name cards to ribbon so that children can wear them round their necks. Fill the basket with cushions to represent a nest.
- Read *Owl Babies* to the children.
- Talk about the illustration depicting the owl babies first realising their mother has gone (spread 2).
- Ask the children how they would feel if they woke up to find an important adult gone. Explain that thinking about our feelings helps us to understand how others might feel in the same situation.
- Divide the class into three, and allocate a baby owl to each group.
- Invite the groups to discuss how their owl might feel after discovering Owl Mother has gone. Suggest that they think of questions to ask the owl about this, and to write them on an individual whiteboard.
- Invite the children to sit in their groups around the 'owl nest'. Ask each group to choose someone to be an owl baby sitting in the nest wearing the name card of their allocated owl.
- Invite groups to take turns to ask their nominated owl one of the questions on their whiteboard.

Differentiation

Support: Ask children to think of single words to describe the owl's feelings. ('unhappy', 'worried')
Extension: Invite the owls to swap their name cards so that they are answering questions about a different owl's feelings.

How to make owl baby puppets

- Follow these instructions and make your own owl baby puppets.

What you will need:

- Owl templates
- Scissors
- Glue
- Sticky tape
- White card
- Six googly eyes
- Yellow felt
- White wool
- Three lengths of dowelling about 20 centimetres long (thin sticks)

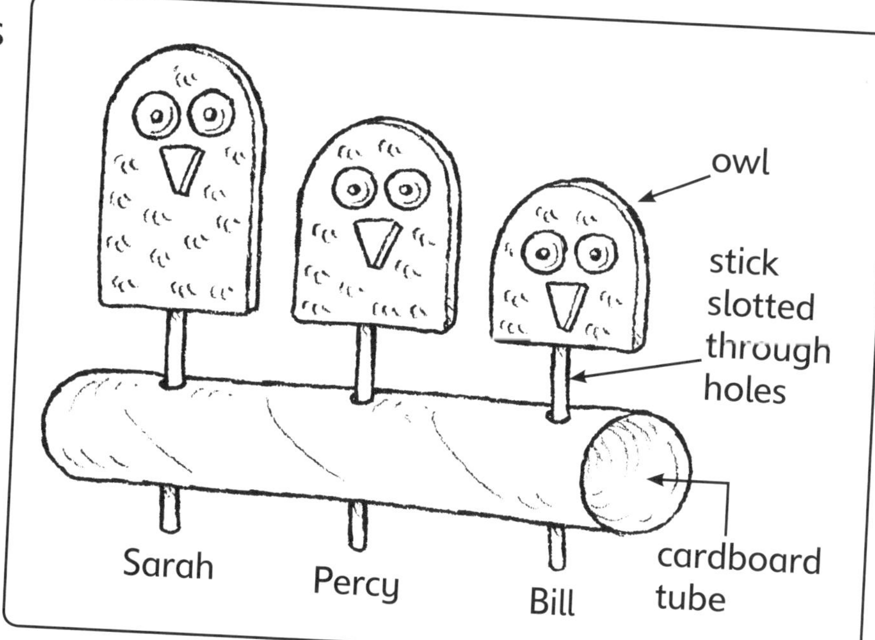

Instructions:

1. Cut out the three owl shapes on printable page 'Owl templates'.
2. Use these as templates to make three owl shapes out of card.
3. Glue or tape a stick to the bottom of the card as a handle.
4. Cut white wool into small pieces to make feathers.
5. Stick the wool feathers all over each owl.
6. Add eyes and a beak made from yellow felt.

GET WRITING

1. Sensing answers

Objective

To discuss what they have written with the teacher or other children.

What you need

Copies of *Owl Babies*, woodland access or examples of woodland vegetation, media resources 'Owl nests', 'Perching owls' and 'Night sounds', photocopiable page 29 'Owl Mother uses her senses', whiteboards.

What to do

- Read *Owl Babies* before recalling the lesson 'Sounds of the night' (page 22). Discuss how a woodland environment might affect all five senses.
- Go for a woodland walk and talk about what the children see, hear, smell and touch. Alternatively, explore a selection of vegetation from woodland.
- Revisit the film clips and images in media resources 'Owl nests', 'Perching owls' and 'Night sounds'. Discuss things owls might see when flying at night.
- Display photocopiable page 29 'Owl Mother uses her senses'. Read the instructions and discuss possible answers to the first question.
- Divide the class into groups of five, each with the photocopiable sheet and five whiteboards. They write the name of a different sense on each board.
- Suggest that groups discuss each question together, writing the things that Owl Mother sees, hears, smells, tastes and touches on their different boards.
- Bring the class together to share their words. Then children complete individual copies of the sheet, making sure their answers are complete sentences.
- Share the completed pages back in groups, asking children to discuss what they have written.

Differentiation

Support: Ask children to answer the first three questions only.
Extension: Invite children to compose a paragraph describing how Owl Mother uses her senses at night.

2. Owl Mother's note

Objectives

To say out loud what they are going to write about.

What you need

Copies of *Owl Babies*, printable page 'Owl Mother's note'.

Cross-curricular link

PSHE

What to do

- Read *Owl Babies*. Ask children for evidence that Owl Mother left without telling her babies where she was going. (The babies discuss where she might be.)
- Consider whether the owl babies would have felt better if they had known where their mother was. Encourage children to share experiences of adults going out without telling them, for example, waking up to find a babysitter looking after them. How did this make them feel? Would they have been happier if they had known their parents were going out?
- Suggest that the babies might have been happier if Owl Mother had left a note in the nest explaining her plans and whereabouts. Discuss the sort of information she should include in such a note.
- Display printable page 'Owl Mother's note' and ask for suggestions to complete each sentence, for example, reminding Sarah to look after her brothers.
- Divide the children into pairs, with a copy of the printable page per child, so partners can share what they plan to write.
- Ask individuals to complete their copies.
- Bring the class together to share examples of finished notes and comment on their likely effectiveness in reassuring the babies.

Differentiation

Support: Focus on completing the first and last sentences of the note only.
Extension: Invite children to compose their own Owl Mother's note without referring to the printable page.

3. My hunting diary

Objectives

To spell the days of the week.

What you need

Media resources 'Owls in flight' and 'Tawny owls', diary, camera, video camera, photocopiable page 30 'My hunting diary', whiteboards.

Cross-curricular links

Computing, science

What to do

- Recall discussions about Owl Mother's likely actions when she left her babies alone.
- Establish the meanings of 'hunting' and 'prey'. Explore the images and clips of owls hunting and catching prey in media resources 'Owls in flight' and 'Tawny owls', and on the internet. Make a list together of the sort of prey Owl Mother might bring home.
- Ask children to think of different methods of recalling events, for example, taking photographs and films, and writing diaries. Pass around a diary and discuss how it might be used to record events.
- Explore a camera and video camera and consider how they work. Then ask children to imagine images and events Owl Mother might capture if she had recording equipment.
- Display photocopiable page 30 'My hunting diary' and read the example entry. Suggest this might be a suitable way for Owl Mother to record her hunting expeditions.
- Ask the children to write the days of the week on their whiteboards in order. Now write them on the board so they can self-check the order and spelling.
- Divide the children into pairs, with a photocopiable sheet per child. Encourage partners to discuss ideas before completing their own page.
- Choose children to show and read their finished pages. Then ask the class to decide which Owl Mother had the most interesting hunting week.

4. Tell the story

Objective

To begin to form lower-case letters in the correct direction, starting and finishing in the right place; to form capital letters.

What you need

Copies of *Owl Babies*, interactive activity 'Sort the sentences', scissors, writing tools, art materials.

Cross-curricular link

Art and design

What to do

- Read *Owl Babies* together to revise the sequence of events.
- Display screen 1 of interactive activity 'Sort the sentences' and read the instructions.
- Revise rules for starting a sentence with a capital letter and finishing with a full stop. Explain that knowing these rules will help them to sort the sentences.
- Read the words along the first row. Decide which group of words will start the sentence (starting with a capital). Drag it to the first box. Now find the last group (ending in a full stop) and drag it to the end box. Drag the remaining group to the middle box. Read the sentence you have made together to check that it makes sense.
- Ask the children to complete the activity in pairs. Once they have finished, they should print their work and cut out the sentences they have created. Explain that the sentences should now be sequenced to tell the *Owl Babies* story.
- Once the children have ordered their sentences, and checked that the story makes sense, they should write it out. Emphasise the importance of forming letters correctly, and allow time to decorate work with illustrations or patterns.
- Display the finished stories and invite someone to judge the best presentation and handwriting.

5. Woodland family stories

Objectives

To read aloud their writing clearly enough to be heard by their peers and the teacher.

What you need

Copies of *Owl Babies*, printable page 'My woodland family story plan', whiteboards.

What to do

- Read *Owl Babies* to the children and ask them to identify the owl family members. Explain that you would like them to write a similar story about a family of woodland creatures.
- Display the story plan on printable page 'My woodland family story plan'. Discuss how plans help when writing stories.
- Invite title suggestions and write the class choice in the 'Title' box, for example, 'Bat Babies'.
- Discuss possible characters and consider whether there will be one or two parents. Suggest that children think of character names and write examples in the boxes. Choose children to write adjectives describing each character in the boxes.
- Briefly discuss suitable story language to start and finish the story. Invite suggestions for events that happen in the middle.
- Divide the class into groups to discuss ideas, using the plan as guidance and jotting down favourite words on whiteboards.
- Provide individuals with a copy of the page to complete, using their whiteboard notes to recall ideas. Once they are satisfied with their plan, ask them to write their story.
- Bring the class together to listen to individual stories. Emphasise the need for writers to read loudly and clearly so that everyone can hear.

Differentiation

Support: Concentrate on writing a single character description and reading it to the class.
Extension: Invite children to include dialogue, and to read this expressively.

6. Satisfying sequels

Objective

To sequence sentences to form short narratives.

What you need

Copies of *Owl Babies*, books from a series about the same character (for example, *The Lighthouse Keeper* series by Ronda and David Armitage), printable page '*Owl Babies* sequel'.

Cross-curricular link

Mathematics

What to do

- Read *Owl Babies*. Explain that some authors write several books about the same character(s) and show examples. Explain the word 'sequel' as a story that follows on from another, or has the same characters experiencing different events.
- Suggest that children write an *Owl Babies* sequel, about when the characters are older. Ask questions to stimulate ideas, for example: *What will happen when the owl babies are old enough to leave their nest? What dangers await them?*
- Discuss possible titles such as 'Let's fly!'.
- Encourage the children to discuss whether the characters will have changed at all. Consider whether to introduce new characters.
- Suggest including an exciting event, such as the owl babies getting lost in the woods.
- Display printable page 'Owl Babies sequel' and read it together. Revise appropriate story language, especially for openings and endings, and focus on the importance of sequencing sentences.
- Ask children to suggest five favourite *Owl Babies* words and write these in the bottom box.
- Suggest that the children discuss and write plans in pairs before writing individual sequels.
- Bring the class together to share their sequels.

Differentiation

Support: Ask children to focus on just completing the plan.

Owl Mother uses her senses

- The owls ask how Owl Mother uses her senses at night.
- Write Owl Mother's answer in the box beside each question.

Sarah Mummy, what do you see when you go out without us?	**Owl Mother**
Percy Mummy, what do you hear while you are flying in the woods?	**Owl Mother**
Bill Mummy, what do you smell?	**Owl Mother**
Percy Mummy, do you taste any of the food you bring back for us?	**Owl Mother**
Bill Mummy, what do you touch?	**Owl Mother**
Sarah Mummy, which senses do you use most when you are out flying?	**Owl Mother**

My hunting diary

- Write the days of the week in the first column.
- Draw a picture of the prey in the second column.
- Write a sentence about where you caught the prey in the third column.

Day	Picture of the prey I caught	Where I caught it
Sunday		I caught the worm in a field as it wriggled out of its burrow.

1. Alphabetical order

Objective

To name the letters of the alphabet in order.

What you need

Charts and friezes depicting upper- and lower-case letters, interactive activity 'Alphabetical order'.

What to do

- Revise letter names and alphabetical order by asking the children to read out the letters by name, and in order, from alphabet charts/friezes.
- Instruct the children to close their eyes and listen while you call out a letter name. Challenge them to say the name of the letter that comes before it, and the one that comes after it. Ask them to open their eyes and check their answer by locating the letter on the chart/frieze.
- Display screen 1 of interactive activity 'Alphabetical order' and explain that this activity has words from the story in a random order and that they are going to put them in alphabetical order. Work through the first row together to ensure that children understand what is required of them.
- Discuss strategies for words beginning with the same initial letters, and the same two initial letters.
- Ask the children to complete the activity individually. (If they need to wait for access, suggest that pairs of children arrange the words from a chosen story line into alphabetical order.) Allow time for individuals to complete the activity before bringing the class together to share responses.

Differentiation

Support: Assess children on their ability to complete screens 1 and 2 where the words all start with different letters.

2. Grammatical terminology

Objective

To use the grammatical terminology in English Appendix 2 in discussing their writing.

What you need

Copies of *Owl Babies*, interactive activity 'Grammatical terminology', individual whiteboards.

What to do

- Revise the grammatical terminology 'noun', 'adjective' and 'verb' by reading out suitable sentences from *Owl Babies* and asking children to identify examples of these words. Assess their understanding by asking for explanations for their answers. If there is any confusion, reinforce the definition of these terms by making up simpler sentences that make the meaning clearer.
- Continue revision using interactive activity 'Grammatical terminology'. Complete the first example as a class so that children understand what is required of them before asking the children to complete the activity individually.
- Bring the class together to discuss results.
- Now ask children to work in pairs to compose a sentence containing at least one noun, verb and adjective. They should then write this sentence on their whiteboard, adding 'N', 'V' and 'A' above the appropriate words.
- Suggest that the pairs form groups of six to share their sentences and discuss their choice of words. Encourage children to use the correct terminology as they talk about their sentences.
- Assess the objective by listening to children's language as they work in pairs and groups.

Differentiation

Support: Invite children to complete the first three activity sentences only, and talk with them about their word choices.
Extension: Ask pairs of children to choose sentences from *Owl Babies* and identify the nouns, adjectives and verbs together.

3. True or false?

Objective

To apply phonic knowledge and skills as the route to decode words.

What you need

Extract 3, interactive activity 'True or false?'.

What to do

- Display Extract 3. Read each fact together, pausing to decode words as necessary.
- Revise grapheme-phoneme correspondences (GPCs) already taught by focusing on one statement, for example, 'Some owls even eat worms, small birds and fish'. Underline the grapheme for a particular phoneme, for example, 'ir' ('birds'), and then ask for examples of different words that have the same GPC ('girl', 'shirt'). Now ask for words with alternative graphemes for the same phoneme ('perched', 'church').
- Display interactive activity 'True or false?' and read the first statement together. Ask children to make a joint decision about whether it is true or false, and then click on their answer.
- Ask the children to read the word 'nocturnal' by breaking it down into separate syllables, and 'day' by identifying the vowel digraph 'ay'. Identify the different graphemes that have been used to create this phoneme in the words 'wait' and 'date'. Do the same with other statements if time permits.
- Provide individuals with a copy of Extract 3 and access to 'True or false?' to complete this activity.
- Bring the class together to discuss their work.
- Assess the objective during revision discussions and while individuals complete the interactive activity.

Differentiation

Support: Provide support with reading the activity screen where necessary.
Extension: Ask children to compose their own owl fact sheets, along with 'True or false?' statements, to challenge their peers.

4. Past or present?

Objective

To re-read what they have written to check that it makes sense; to use the present and past tenses correctly and consistently.

What you need

Interactive activity 'Past or present?'.

What to do

- Revise the meanings of 'tense', 'past' and 'present' by writing a simple sentence about the owl babies on the board, for example, 'The babies live in a hole'. Ask children to identify the tense, using appropriate questions to clarify your meaning if necessary, for example: *Is this happening now or in the past?*
- Invite children to convert your sentence into the past tense and discuss how they did this.
- Make up sentences in both the past and present tense, then ask the children to swap the tense. If children are ready, introduce examples of the progressive form, for example, 'The owls are living in a hole.' Take away the word 'are' and ask if this still makes sense.
- Display screen 1 of interactive activity 'Past or present?' and read the instructions together.
- Read the first sentence and choose the correct word from the drop-down menu together. Read it again, checking whether it makes sense and is in the correct tense.
- Invite children to complete the activity individually, emphasising the need to read each sentence after completion to check that it makes sense.
- Assess the objective through the activity and oral answers given during discussions.

Differentiation

Support: Avoid the four sentences involving the progressive form when completing the activity.